Lucky
to be Alive

A Love Story

Wendy E. Shepard

[signature: Wendy E. Shepard]

San Juan Valley Press
Friday Harbor,
Washington USA
2012

*For Colleen and Harvey,
with gratitude,
Wendy & Jeff*

Lucky to be Alive: A Love Story
Copyright © 2012 by Wendy E. Shepard

Published in the U.S.A. by
    San Juan Valley Press LLC
    P.O. Box 918
    Friday Harbor, WA 98250
    www.sanjuanvalleypress.com

Cover: Charcoal drawing of Lucky and Valley photo
        Copyright © 2012 by Jeff Brash

Author photo by Cynthia Blair Miller

Cover design and interior layout by
    Ian Byington, By Design

ISBN 978-0-9851363-0-7

Library of Congress Control Number: 2012937835

Printed in the U.S.A.

First Edition

for

Jeff and Lucky

with

gratitude and love

Author's Note

Lucky to be Alive was a surprise. It spilled out in its present form, a narrative poem that reads like prose. Originally, I thought it would be a short story, but it never worked. My training in musical theatre taught me that a song appears when the feeling becomes too intense for words. Lucky's story is one of feelings so strong that it has to be a song.

For readers who want to know about the structure: except for the Haiku poems that introduce each chapter (17 syllables in three lines, divided 5-7-5), the structure came from my own whimsy, emerging as I played with Nature's rhythms. Its stanzas have fourteen lines, and its "feet," or beats per line, change with the seasons: four beats for Winter, five for Spring, six for Summer, five for Autumn, and four beats for Another Winter.

Formal poetry might have various names for all these elements of structure, but a Border Collie is anything but formal. In Lucky's honor, this piece simply follows his lead, cheering him on during his quest for a happy life.

Lucky to be Alive
A Love Story

Table of Contents

Chapter One
Winter 1

Chapter Two
Spring 15

Chapter Three
Summer 29

Chapter Four
Autumn 43

Chapter Five
Another Winter 63

Lucky, the Amazing Border Collie
Charcoal drawing by Jeff Brash

Chapter One

WINTER reminds Life that vast promises are still to be discovered.

Half-hearted rain clouds
wandered through the skies, sometimes
giving way to teasing sunbreaks,
as weather forecasters wistfully called
the promises of spring. "One day,
but not yet," whispered the mist
to those who listened, a reminder to dwell
in all that was. The clouds heard
and wondered why they were unwelcome.
Did bodies not remember that they
were mostly water? Were they forgetting
to raise their arms to the sky and catch
the gift of water on their thirsty tongues?
The raindrops longed, *yearned*, to be welcome.

Seeds rested in the island valley.
It would take the rays of a warmer sun
to awaken them to new life.
No one knew whether or not
seeds felt thankful for the water that rocked them
in their beds, or valued the farmers who tilled
a path for healthy growth, or were glad
to be useful, serving as food for animals,
and people, who often gave thanks to the seeds.
No one really knew anything,
or rather, everyone knew all
that was and is and will be, but the knowledge
was buried within a forgotten past
that longed, *yearned*, to be remembered.

Lucky spent his life remembering.
During a bright, joyous sunbreak
that painted the wings of the seagulls a shimmering
white and the fields a brilliant green,
creating a stunning contrast to the dark
gray skies above and making
people smile and neglect their complaints,
Lucky was born in the Land of Grateful.
Swans feeding on luxuriant grasses
in the ponds and fields of their winter home,
bald eagles carrying branches
to their nests in the tall, windblown firs,
Holstein dairy cows lunching
on leftover hay from the summer's crop–

their voices called out the news
while orcas sang, as whales can,
to welcome this dog, a Border Collie,
black and white like them, their neighbor.
The black and white sheep were silent,
ignoring the whole event (had been herded
one too many times, perhaps).
They continued to graze, cropping the grass
better than mechanical mowers
or other such human inventions.
Sunbreaks had their jobs as well,
heating the glass windows of the farmhouse,
helping the mother dog warm
her puppies until their coats grew thick.

Tumbling about with the newborns, enshrined
in their tiny hearts, were Dreamers, keeping them
company at night and helping them remember
during the day what they wanted
to dream alive. Milk came first,
that irresistible scent from beyond
Lucky's tightly closed eyes.
The rest would wait until the eyes
opened and the puppy began to walk,
away from his loving and worried mother
and then (on a day when the farmer came in
from the fields and left the door ajar)
over the low wooden frame
of his pen and onto the door sill.

It was Lucky's first exuberant *Wow!*
Few ever forget the first,
the heart leaping to meet love,
or beauty, or the onset of a grand adventure.
Lucky's bark was the sound of destiny
unfolding with his first glimpse of rain.
It swept across the valley to fields
that had once nurtured strawberries and peas,
crops long gone, forsaken
when human engineering provided
mainland farmers with irrigation.
Their trains sent produce to markets
for less money than island farmers
paid to haul their wares over water.

Down the stairs, soft fur
rippling in the wind, Lucky gingerly
took his first steps outside.
They led to an unexpected friendship
with drops of rain that fell on his nose,
then on the tongue which had fallen from his mouth
at his first smile, a pleasurable sensation,
stretching the lips to greet the fun.
He played his first game: guessing
where the raindrops would fall next,
tongue extended to catch as many
as he could, while his raindrop friends skipped
and bounced on the ground to celebrate a creature
that actually wanted to play with them.

Clambering up a hillock, Lucky
saw the distant body of water
that led to the towering mountains beyond.
The raindrops fell as far as Lucky could
see, as if wanting to touch everything
they could reach. Cooperating rainclouds
raced ahead, for time is short
to fulfill a mission, one that Lucky
shared with the raindrops. He was a born
explorer who would inhale as much experience
as was doggedly possible. He would follow the rain
that softened the earth, uncovering scents
more vital than those in his pen
of newspaper and rough-hewn siding.

His sister became his constant companion.
They discovered the woods, the smell of pines,
raccoons that ransacked the garbage cans
of human neighbors, deer heavy
with fawns and dreams of dessert such as tulips
and roses and tender leaves of bushes,
all awaiting the spring to come.
Birds sang their winter songs,
composing variations when moved
to build their nests, but not yet.
Crows, who liked a romp as much as
the raindrops, cawed their jokes and stories
of the forest to any who would listen and laugh
and dance with these comical, fanciful birds.

Lucky and his sister played with them all.
Then she was gone. So were the others,
and the woods, fields, raindrops. Oh *no*,
so were the raindrops. And the farmhouse, the farmer,
his wife reading stories to her children and Lucky,
once-upon-a-time tales
showing the young the workings of life
in which everything happened only once,
never quite in the same way,
never quite in the same place,
never quite at the same moment,
each raindrop, every single
something with its own unique purpose,
with its own way of being alive.

Where were they? Lucky whimpered.
Dreamer raced to his side, startled.
Lucky was an active, outdoor pup,
intent on pursuing his whims at his pleasure,
needing no guidance, or reminders
of plans to hatch. No worries to calm,
no mouth turned down, no sadness slowing
his jaunty gait. No wonder
that Dreamer's attention often wavered,
that he visited with other Dreamers. His job,
he thought, was easy. Till now,
for Lucky was in a shelter for homeless animals,
surrounded by wires twisting and turning,
woven into a confining cage.

Dreamer berated himself. *How* could he
neglect his duty and allow this monstrous
change in Lucky's life? How *could* he?
How had he been so remiss?
Why was it all gone, gone, gone?
Dreamer shook himself, like Lucky
after a running game with the raindrops.
Not everything is in a Dreamer's control.
In times of terrible trauma, the best
that Dreamers can do is to let their charges
know that they are not alone,
that everything changes, all is temporary,
once-upon-a-time. "Lucky,
hang on, hang on, hang on, hang on."

Lucky heard Dreamer over the din
of yelping, whining, growling dogs.
Who was that? He saw nothing.
"I am your Dreamer. Go to sleep."
He sang a lullaby so sweet that
Lucky followed it into slumber,
twitching, fitful, hearing but not
understanding Dreamer's instruction
to dream his future alive. How?
"By letting go, Lucky," said Dreamer,
"allow what you want to do to speak."
Lucky did not want to listen
to the shelter's desperate noises, or to sleep
on the cold cement on the floor of a cage.

Easy to know what he did not want,
harder to hear what his future desired.
Such is the winter of life, the seeds
of what is to be barely stirring.
Young ones, humans included,
sit in the midst of their changing selves
with no clear sense of direction,
attentive to any hints that might
guide them to their destiny, discovering
along the way that life's journey
is little more than a guessing game.
Lucky awoke with images of his mother,
sister, brothers, farm family.
That was the only future he wanted.

Explanations of the seeming impossible
were beyond Dreamer's expertise,
for the spirit's sensibilities do not
understand that people let money,
pieces of green paper, determine
the outcome of their uncertain lives.
Lucky's human companions had to move
to the mainland to get enough money to feed them?
The land that grew such healthy food
was impoverished, said the bank full of money?
Nature gave freely, with generous abundance.
Had banks forgotten this law that sustained
life on Earth? Including them?
It was nearly impossible to explain.

Dreamer tried. His description of money
made Lucky gag; his early attempts
to eat the pages of the children's books
were still a disagreeable memory.
Why would a person want paper?
Lucky shivered under the loss
of his warm home. Dreamer sighed,
wanting to see him untroubled,
but sometimes life is excruciating and sad
and sometimes that is all that is.
No consolation exists
except an instinctual compassion that fights
its way to the conscious mind, reminding it that
life's wheel will turn around.

And turn it did, slowly at first,
nurturing inner knowing in Lucky
that taught him how to follow the wheel,
how to trust that his best interests
lay in its supportive, lively hub.
Dreamer could not rescue him,
could not change things by himself;
Lucky and Dreamer were equal partners
in both the waking and sleeping realms.
Lucky had to lift his heavy head
to do his part, remain true
to the sunbreak of his birth, shine through the clouds,
manage to wag his tail and smile
at the shelter people, cheerful souls

who smiled in return and brought him food,
the aroma comforting after hours of smelling
disinfectants and strange dogs.
He wagged and smiled at each child
who arrived after school to give him a walk.
Every outing was an adventure, for Lucky
was young and his nose so new
that he could spend ten minutes
sniffing out the secrets of a fern.
When walking past the nearby airfield,
a small plane magically flew
up to the sky, making a noise
like no other bird, a sound that had caused him
many a shudder as he cowered indoors.

Now, as he looked and listened, the sound
became the eager call of flight,
loud here, then soft away.
That was all. His fear dissolved,
as fears do when facing them makes them
flee, tails between their legs.
Where was the airplane going? Lucky
wanted to follow it. Fly with the raindrops;
he missed them more than anything.
No young ones took Lucky for walks
when it rained; he often heard the raindrops
on the metal roof asking for him,
their message distinct, insistent, friendly:
"Lucky, will you not come out and play?"

Dreamer carried Lucky that night
to the rolling fields of sodden grasses
that led to the bay, to the mountains, and back
to Lucky's domain of woods and farms.
In the morning, the young dog awoke
with a rare bark: *that* is what he wanted!
To be free to play with the rain in the valley!
No cage or leash. It was so simple.
From then on, Lucky inhabited
his transient shelter with a peaceful heart.
An unshakable vision of what his future
held summoned the patience for the day
when it would appear. And at night he lived
that vision in dream after glorious dream,

covering every inch of the land
finding, finding...that would be shown,
when the time was right. Soon, he knew.
And soon it was that a great big
sheep farmer with a great big
smile stood in front of Lucky,
whose tail found a will of its own,
wagging with abandon while the sheep farmer
laughed a great big laugh,
then walked on as Lucky watched him
move toward the office desk.
Dogs yapped, but the farmer kept going,
turning once to look at Lucky,
who gave him the gift of his sunbreak smile.

Then the cage was gone. Lucky
was on a leash, then off the leash,
then on the farmer's truck bed,
the rain on his face welcoming him,
laughingly drenching him. The Holstein cows,
and even the sheep, the trumpeter swans,
the eagles and orcas, all announced
the triumphant return of Lucky, the dog,
black and white, just like them.
"How could I resist a Border Collie
with a sunbreak smile?" the farmer asked
his benevolent wife, who gave Lucky his name:
"You are lucky to be alive," she said,
and sent him outside to play in the rain.

Chapter Two

SPRING invites desire

to help Life solve the puzzle

of making choices.

Sunbreak yellow heralded spring on the island:
daffodils, forsythia, grape ivy–and dandelions,
the scourge of some human gardeners who wanted
their lawns a meticulous green, who called them ugly.
Yet the intrepid flowers bloomed anyway.
"It does not matter," they said, "if someone cannot
see your beauty. You have to know your own,
open your arms to all about you
in order to brighten your day and that of another."
Lucky was color-blind, some people said
with arrogance, for they needed any excuse to say
that they were the most superior living beings
while the truth, as all dandelions knew,
is that all life on Earth is of equal worth

Some people isolated others because
of the color of their skin, but some were color-blind
in that way, knowing others were equals.
"Every creature has its own way
of perceiving the world," Dreamer told Lucky,
reminding him of his profound sense of smell,
thousands of times stronger than that of people.
"Your own gifts are equally magical."
People who could not comprehend equality
started conflicts and wars, trying to prove
their greater importance, running a human race,
trying to win. To win? A very puzzling
pursuit since, as all dandelions knew,
every one, every thing, is a winner.

"You see colors, but differently from people,"
said Dreamer. Lucky was confused. What was color?
Dreamer tried to describe the delicate palette
of spring, but finally had to admit defeat.
Not spirit nor intellect could possibly capture
the color of a sun, a rainbow, or the dandelion seeds
that tickled Lucky's nose and made him sneeze.
Lucky was almost a year old by now,
about seven human years, the time
when children go to school to learn about
their gifts and how to use them well. Lucky
wanted to roam, but school was necessary.
If he did not respect his own talents, he certainly
would not know how to respect those of others.

Lucky's school was based on the relationship
between people and dogs, from the human point of view.
Obedience came first. Lucky excelled,
to the surprise of those who knew his independence,
for transcending his willful ways was a desire, like Dreamer's,
to spread happiness wherever he went.
The exercises were easy for Lucky, especially
heeling to the commands of the farmer's wife, for at night
he stayed by her side while she cooked dinner, drooling
mightily at the enticing aromas of roasting
cow and sheep and pig and fresh vegetables.
When he finished first in his canine class,
the farmer's reward was savory scraps from his plate,
which Lucky downed with gulps of appreciation.

The dog had earned a vacation. What better
one than to scamper about with occasional raindrops,
fewer during springtime, as if they, too,
needed a rest after a winter of serving
trees, sleeping seeds, and deep channels
that led to ponds and lakes, replenishing the store
of island water for spring and summer farming.
Lucky followed the rain through fields and woods
and, once, onto a road while chasing a raindrop
to catch it before it reached the ground, not
seeing the truck with frightened metal brakes
screaming a warning. Too late. Once
upon this dreadful time, the first time
his body knew pain. Not his favorite first.

He crawled under a bush, as animals tend
to do when sensing death coming for them.
Strong arms surprised him, lifted him up
to the gray light of a wet spring day,
to the familiar sound of the farm truck's motor,
to the smell of the antiseptic of the doctor's office,
to panic. Oh, *no*, was he back at the shelter?
Gentle hands moved over his shoulder
and leg, soft voices whispered in his ear,
not shelter voices, the farmer and his wife.
Lucky drifted off, staying with Dreamer
for a few days while the farm couple waited
for life or death. For sometimes Nature's plan
decides, and sometimes that is all that is.

Dreamer watched over Lucky, who awoke
only to lick the pain away, maybe
remembering his mother's healing tongue (akin
to people kissing a hurt, trying to comfort
body and soul as mothers tend to do).
Lucky became stronger, the reason why
a mystery to Dreamer, his physical side a marvel
beyond his grasp, a tiny seed that grew
to drink its mother's milk and bound through fields.
What fun to have a body! Even in pain,
what solace in a healing touch! Wholeness returned,
no hint of a limp, except when courting love
after misbehavior, sympathy always
thawing anger over a chewed slipper.

How, Lucky asked Dreamer one night,
how was it that his wishes came into being?
His desire to leave the shelter to play with the raindrops,
healing after the accident when he might have died,
both occurring without even trying?
How did that happen? Dreamer did not know.
It might have been, he said, that Lucky lived
his dream so deeply, even in the shelter feeling the
raindrops fall, letting the wet grass
tickle his underside, becoming the dream until
the dream became his life. Might have been.
As for when he should die: this was not his time.
Did an inner knowing of destiny to fulfill
foster healing? Make dreams come true?

Wow! It was Lucky's second big Wow.
Dreamer barely heard, concerned about
the dreams that might not come true.
Every life had meaning of its very own;
some dreams might not apply.
Dreamer did not tell Lucky this,
for the young dog was still fragile in body
and spirit. Besides, Dreamer was humble enough
to question his own authority to judge dreams.
What dream was right, and what wrong?
Either could come true, but always in a way,
perhaps, that would impart beneficial learning.
Dreamer had to have faith in the process
of living if his waking half was to do the same.

Illness brings quiet, meditation
that encourages new ideas to show their faces.
Lucky left his blanket to go outside
where he heard the Spring Symphony, all its parts
playing in unison, inwardly knowing that they
had Nature's power to create music, so they did:
frogs and whales singing; bald eagles
calling to each other when gathering a feast
of mole or vole; black and white cows
mooing encouragement to newborn calves;
bleating from black and white sheep while lambs
pranced; and ravens, glossy black, adding
their chortles. Lucky listened all spring,
his own sound missing. He seldom barked.

"Why?" asked Dreamer once, for never had
he known a dog to be so quiet. Silence.
Dreamer assured him he did not have to bark.
Just wondered if he had a reason. Silence.
A bewildered silence, not born of anxiety.
Dreamer felt comfortable with Lucky's way,
but he wished to know more about the waking world.
Was Lucky shy? Did he feel he had little to say?
Did he not know the value of every voice?
No time for questions, for life's wheel
turned again. Another school began,
with the farmer, for Lucky was a Border Collie
whose job, humans thought, was to herd sheep.
Like those of people, his school was for basic skills.

Lucky started late because of his injuries.
Having no use for excuses, he soon
caught up with the younger dogs, outdid them,
graduated once more first in his class.
Not that he knew what it meant, except that the farmer
was pleased and that was enough. Not that his schooling
was evident in the farmhouse, especially obedience; toys
of rubber and rope for chewing lay dormant,
better to gnaw on socks, shoes, blankets
imbued with the earthy scent of the people he loved.
Dreamer intervened. Following his nose,
his instinct, was the key to finding the path of his life,
but his nose must not cause others trouble.
Compatibility within a group was everything.

"Such is the springtime of life," taught Dreamer,
liking the sound of his voice, forgetting Lucky,
"learning about relationship with others,
how to compromise when what we want
causes another suffering. It is a time of finding
our balance, teetering and tottering between our desires
and the needs of others, true to our own purpose
but honoring that of the many, the well-being
of the individual and the group, equal in value...."
Lucky's stare made Dreamer pause.
Embarrassed by his own rambling, he fell silent.
How very pompous. How superfluous.
This lover of music, this gentle dog,
needed no lecture on how to behave.

What was the role of a Dreamer? He did not know.
Teacher? Sometimes. Best friend? Always.
He might have more to learn, he sensed, than Lucky,
finished with school and out in the field with the sheep.
The farmer gave him the right commands to herd them,
the sheep bleated, but Lucky sat down. And listened.
Their music was a favorite part of the Spring Symphony;
to interrupt would be rude, so Lucky smiled,
inviting the farmer to join him on the grass.
The farmer, nonplussed, repeated commands,
his insistence a mystery to Lucky, whose face sagged.
Few creatures fully comprehend
another's inner workings. Lucky and the farmer,
and certainly the surprised sheep, were no exception.

Since love is not an earned thing, Lucky
did not have to herd to keep the devotion
of the farmer's family. An additional Border Collie,
however, one that would herd, was a necessity.
Lucky was silent when the new brother arrived,
barking incessantly, trying to tell his story.
Lucky turned away, and finally walked
away. Left the farm, in fact, following
new scents and sounds across the valley,
usually arriving back at the house for dinner,
but even that became a sometime visit
when he caught delicious critters of the field instead.
Lucky was three by now, twenty-one
in human years, a time to explore the world.

But Dreamer worried. Human Dreamers had mentioned
that when new children come into a family,
older children could become jealous, as if parents
had not enough love to go around.
The bounty of Nature escaped their young notice,
as did the infinite forms of life, every
blade of grass different but each receiving
sunshine and rain in equal measure.
"Do you feel unloved?" Dreamer asked.
No, Lucky did not. He tried in vain
to uncover his feelings. "Maybe," Dreamer continued,
"you feel that you are less than successful, knowing that
you cannot do jobs people expect of you?"
Lucky knew it was not that he could not; he would not.

Herding sheep was a gigantic yawn to Lucky,
as was Fetch, a game dogs played and played.
Lucky did not want to repeat himself,
he wanted to listen to the changing Spring Symphony.
Suddenly, a moment of clarity: the new dog
barked. He barked, hurting Lucky's ears,
drowning out the gentle sounds of spring.
"I think I see," said Dreamer. "It is like the shelter."
No. Not quite. Lucky slumped.
Clarity had flown. Crossly, he muttered to his friend,
"You do not know anything, do you!"
Dreamer slumped with him. "No, I do not."
Lucky softened. "It is all right, Dreamer.
I do not either. Wait! I do!" He knew.

His realizations came in a rush. The dog
had barked and had been chosen anyway,
had barked at home and even so was loved.
Dreamer was right, shelter memories
flooded back, people avoiding the yappers,
choosing quiet dogs. Lucky thought
he had it figured out, so he was quiet
and smiled a lot. When he went to the sheep farm,
he kept quiet, so that they would not return him
to the shelter. So many times he had wanted
to bark, and kept it in for fear that he would lose
everything. Dreamer prodded him gently. "Do you think
that the farmer would have sent you away?"
An image of the jolly farmer's face appeared.

It was an expansive image. No, of course not,
he had not returned the new dog to the shelter.
His manner showed that he cared for both dogs,
equally, though they were very different.
Lucky could have barked and barked and barked.
It was all right to *bark*! He had not known.
Wow! It was Lucky's third big Wow.
"You are not alone," Dreamer assured him.
"Human children are often afraid to speak.
They might say something wrong, or people who matter
to them, like parents, might see that they are not
as perfect as they had hoped, or friends might not
like them because they are different,
not understanding that different is all that is."

Dreamer doubted that the different grasses had
such fears. But, sadly, many
children did, until they finally realized
that the fears were false, that they needed to be
like the dandelions and show themselves
even if others might not like them.
"Dogs need to know that they can speak.
Although," Dreamer added in haste, remembering
Lucky's early years, "it is all right
not to bark, too. If you had barked
all the time, you might have missed the pleasure
of hearing the Spring Symphony. You could teach
the new dog how to listen to it."
"But he is a *dog*!" Lucky barked. "A *dog*!"

The words slipped out, unbidden. Had Lucky
said too much? It appeared not.
Dreamer was just learning about his role,
but one thing was certain: waking sides
needed to trust their own Dreamers. A lively
conversation followed, Dreamer wondering
if Lucky knew he was a dog, and Lucky wondering
what that was, and Dreamer unable to say,
for he could not describe existence. Who can?
Who can describe that whimsical force
residing in every atom, energizing all,
taking any form it desires, resulting in a
world of differences that changes constantly? Who
can explain that to anyone's satisfaction?

For whatever reason, and few know their reasons
for doing anything, and none want to be judged
for their reasons, Lucky wanted a place where he
was the only dog. His forays into the valley
to gather dog cookies from neighbors brought him
to the house of an older Scottish couple who soon
became the last stop on his daily rounds.
Island lore was peppered with Scots clearing
the land to grow crops, cutting trees,
teams of horses and oxen hauling rockboats,
or sleds, that dumped boulders on the northern hilltop.
Since Border Collie history lay partly in Scotland,
time and space collided when Lucky and the Scots
met, ancestors looking over their shoulders, perhaps.

Lucky seldom went to the sheep farm
for meals, although the farmer's wife kindly
fed him whenever he visited them and their children.
The older couple gave him food as well,
so Lucky never went hungry, the supplies
from domestic and wild sources more than enough.
He was saved from becoming rotund by running through
the fields day and night, no matter the weather.
The older couple did not mean to adopt
the friendly dog but the wise farmer, knowing
they were alone and attached to Lucky, and knowing
Lucky's aversion to the other Border Collie,
let them satisfy Lucky's yearning
for a place with only one dog. Himself.

Chapter Three

SUMMER lovingly

frees Life from the boundary

of expectations.

Leaving home for the first time shortens the breath,
sets in motion feelings of excitement, anticipation,
and pure, unmistakable fear. Facing the world
alone, and yet not alone, adrift in a sea
of others, strangers some, or acquaintances, some
becoming lifelong friends-a crowded place,
the future, replete with choices to make, blunders to regret,
surprises to delight, and direction sometimes fogged in.
Lucky spent his early years roaming widely.
The ready companionship that neighbors provided was
     as nourishing
to his heart as their delectable treats were to his apparent
inexhaustible capacity for groceries. The volume of food
was so overwhelming that much would certainly be wasted
if he kept it all for himself. What was he to do?

The beneficence of summer provided him with hints.
Vacationing rain clouds meant clear skies
and sunshine for the land below, and fullness of vegetation.
Every inch of Nature burgeoned to please the senses
and assure the survival of its dependents. Fields abounded
with grasses for fodder and vegetables for island residents,
     and vibrant
flowers offered up both their fragrance and their food.
The bright red crocosmia helped to strengthen
the rufous hummingbirds for their migration south in August.
Bees visited the blue ceanothus blossoms through July.
Circling swallows fed on the bugs that Lucky unwittingly
scattered with his feet as he ran; a great game, he thought.
Then, the realization: he, too, was providing
food for others. But most of the swallows left by September.

Lucky, like all young people, like Border Collies
everywhere, needed a full-time job,
a way to exercise his talents, reveal his purpose,
discover how his life could tell a joyful story.
Young people at that time were enslaved, money
cracking its hurtful whip over their proverbial backs.
Many shunned the adventures waiting just for them
to follow the call of material wealth. Their faithful Dreamers,
caring guides through the maze of worldly chaos,
mourned both the loss of meaning and their primary jobs,
for abandoned Dreamers travel lonely, lackluster roads.
Lucky's Dreamer went to comfort one of them,
quite sure that his own waking side was content.
Obviously, he needed a reminder to stay with his charge.

A tremulous sigh from the sleeping Lucky brought him back.
"Dreamer, where are you?" Lucky began to panic.
When feeling disconnected from the inner Dreamer,
the waking side inhabits a disconsolate space and time,
not always knowing what is missing, knowing only
a dreadful, frightening emptiness. Lucky moaned.
"Lucky, I am here. What do you need?" Another moan.
Dreamer apologized; he was young, like Lucky,
unaware that his waking side needed him so much.
He assured Lucky that he was ever in his heart,
even if his attention wandered, exploring, as Lucky did.
"Exploration is not enough anymore," said Lucky.
Something other than Dreamer was definitely missing inside,
something vague, unformed, calling his name.

Such is the nature of the summer of the soul, a desire
    for completion,
fulfillment, at the very heart of the will to live.
Dreamer wanted to help Lucky unravel the mystery,
but was it beyond his comprehension of the waking side?
"What do you want?" he asked Lucky, who did not know.
Dreamer told him of a wise human adage: to know
where you are going you need to revisit where you have been.
Lucky agreed to look at his beginnings. Night after night,
Dreamer brought him images of that first farm, the children,
the parents, the large vegetable garden. *Oh!* and the rabbits!
Lucky had almost forgotten the rabbits that ate the carrots,
the parsley, the celery, the lettuce, everything in sight!
Did they have to leave because of the rabbits? Lucky had been
too little to chase them. But now? He barked in his sleep.

At sunrise, Lucky started his new job.
It was too late for his first family, but he could help
other farms survive if he did away with rabbits.
The Scottish couple looked on in amazement as Lucky
began a frenzy of sniffing out rabbit holes,
then digging, forcing the rodents into the open field.
It was not long before he caught one, and it was not long
before a strange feeling arose, a sense that something
was watching, waiting. All the hairs on his craned neck
and his tensed, alert back stood straight up.
As Lucky left the injured rabbit to turn around,
down swooped a red-tailed hawk, grabbing
the rabbit and feasting in the field a short distance away.
Was the hawk taking Lucky's job away from him?

Dismayed, then determined, Lucky leapt over the tall grass
and pounced, scaring the hawk away. Then he ate,
without gusto, for hunger was not his motivation.
What was it? He was, for the first time, possessive.
It was an attribute foreign to him, and unwelcome.
Suddenly, a fierce pair of eyes landed before him,
those of a bald eagle, so authoritative
that Lucky backed away and watched him eat with...with
pleasure? Yes, it was indeed. So it was.
Wow! So many Wows lately! Dreamer heard,
and every night sent him dreams of feeding others.
Lucky had the delicate task of rendering the rabbits
immobile, since hawks and eagles preferred live prey.
Turkey vultures cleaned up whatever was left.

The field became known as Lucky's Luncheonette.
Whenever Lucky caught a rabbit, he barked,
alerting his new customers that lunch was ready.
The eagles, hawks, and turkey vultures, appreciative
of the fresh daily specials, became Lucky's friends.
Associates, too, in his work. He sent them to neighboring fields
to help farms flourish. Poisoning rabbits was not
an option for farmers if the land, vegetables, water table,
living things (including themselves) were to be healthy.
Eagles were part of the answer. Their young ones, newly
fledged, still depended on parents for all their meals.
The fields became their school, where they learned to provide
    for themselves.
Lucky barked and barked, rabbit after rabbit, finally
knowing that he had something important to say to the world.

Lucky's new job kept him so busy,
and his hunger so sated, that his visits to the sheep farmer
and the Scottish couple lessened, as visits of young people
to their parents lessen once they enter the workaday world.
Personal relationships can suffer, or rather, change,
as the definition of home changes from time to time.
One day, after the birds of prey had eaten,
a pair of bald eagles, longtime friends of Lucky,
issued a special call. Eagles appeared from every
part of the valley, their children, maybe, or grandchildren.
Was it a celebration? A meeting to plan their September
fishing retreat on the mainland? Or was it just for the fun
of being together? Together. The word resonated in the dog
who had roamed without ties for most of his adult years.

Few trees remained as perches for the eagle clan,
early settlers having removed them to grow their crops.
On this day, the skies were overflowing with eagles
blaring their news, or was it laughing, giddy fledglings
showing off new skills and learning more.
Then a comfortable silence as the family crowded Together
(that word again) among the branches of two firs.
A deeply felt longing filled Lucky's heart
as the eagles flew home to their aeries. Why did they
    have to go fishing?
Their October return seemed far away. The feelings
that washed over Lucky were unfamiliar. "Dreamer?"
Lucky tried to find the words to express how
he felt. "I am all alone," he blurted out.
Dreamer's feelings were hurt; he began to whimper.

"Dreamer? Are you *crying?*" Lucky was startled. "Yes,"
Dreamer admitted. "How could you not know
that you are not alone, that we are Together always?" Lucky
knew, but still he wanted, no, *thirsted*, for something
outside him, that he could touch, smell, like living with
    his sister and brothers
as a puppy, cuddling with his mother in the utility room pen.
The next morning, the piercing whistle of an eagle brought
Lucky's answer: he wanted a *nest!* Not an aerie,
but a *nest!* A place for him and some undefined others.
How to help an outdoor dog find a nest?
A daunting task, thought Dreamer. Lucky slept outside
at the sheep farm, and later, on cold nights, in the garage
of the Scottish couple, but it had a cement floor like that
of the animal shelter, bringing on anxious, troubled dreams.

While Dreamer sought a solution, Lucky slept deeply.
When dream images are lacking, the waking side can only
follow the directives of the heart, opening eyes and mind
to whatever crosses its shadowed path. And so it was
that one day he heard the roar of a large motor
approaching from the road, growing louder, but hidden
    from view.
A feeling of inexplicable anticipation arose,
born of that sudden certainty that heralds wondrous
    unfoldings.
A giant backhoe appeared, carving a curved driveway
into the rocky hilltop, avoiding the tall firs (to the great
relief of the eagles), avoiding as well the spreading pines,
leaving intact the blackberry bushes that provided shelter
for scurrying quail, thorny bushes that left Lucky
unscathed as he fearlessly chased rabbits into and out of them.

Behind the backhoe was a pumpkin-colored pickup truck,
an old Ford that had seen decades of reliable use.
The truck stopped. A bearded man stepped out.
With the driver of the tractor, he walked to
   an electrical hookup
near the road, unaware of Lucky as he trotted behind them,
respectful of their concentration. Lucky spotted a culvert,
a giant pipe in the ditch that looked like a rabbit hole.
The bearded man turned. All he could see was Lucky's
ever-wagging tail protruding from the empty pipe,
head buried as he sniffed for luncheonette supplies.
The backhoe driver knew Lucky and guessed he was hunting
the rabbits that dined every day in the vegetable gardens.
The bearded man shouted into the culvert's other end,
"LUCKY, THERE ARE NO RABBITS HERE!"

With startling speed, Lucky backed out and saw
the man try his best to straighten up but he was
laughing so hard he could barely stand. Seeing
Lucky's sunbreak smile, the widest he had ever produced,
the man swore that the dog laughed, too. It was the first of
many jokes that the two played on each other
as trucks came and went during the construction period.
Unknown to the man, his laugh became a treasured part
of Nature's Symphony and one of Lucky's favorite sounds.
Another *Wow!* To make the man laugh was a job
that made Lucky's heart sing with newfound music.
For this was no ordinary friend. What was he?
He knew only that the man, like him, loved to dig.
A foundation for his future house, ditches for water pipes

and electrical cables, holes for Leland Cypress trees
including ditches for drainage to avoid flooding
    from the rains
of autumn and winter, and a deep, profusely flowing well.
All a mirror for Lucky's digging for rabbits and voles,
all echoing the digging of the early Scottish settlers
over a century earlier, for they, too, had dug
for houses, and drainage for vegetable fields, massive ditches
from the north of the valley to the south, four feet wide,
ten feet deep, filled with rocks the size of
cantaloupes and watermelons, carrying the excess
water down the hill, away from crops, to the sea.
When times collide, it is as if the land has memories
that it passes on from generation to generation,
energetic images that inspire the dreams of inhabitants.

No, this was no ordinary friend. And *food*,
they both loved *food*. The man brought
fellow workers lunch every day: Mexican,
Thai, Chinese, American, Mid-Eastern food
from restaurants in the small town that served the island
with imagination, welcoming all traditions, culling
the freshest from the local farmers. The ambrosial dishes
    made Lucky
dizzy with delight, as did the leavings on the paper plates,
which he scooped up with a tongue like a living,
    breathing shovel.
Some said that dogs should not have onions, or garlic,
or spicy dishes, but the scraps contained every known
food taboo, it seemed, and Lucky ate them all.
He took treats from the human hand with a delicacy
and grace that belied his robust appetite and burly frame.

Lucky even helped with the building of the house, in his way.
He left his pawprint in the electric meter's wet cement.
As Dreamer watched, he asked himself: was Lucky staking
his claim, giving notice that these seven acres
adjoining those of the Scottish couple were his territory,
as was the rest of the sloping valley? Might be.
Was it saying that he was the man's protector? Perhaps so.
Was it Lucky knowing he had found his place? Maybe.
"No," said Lucky later that day. "It was fun!
It made the bearded man laugh! That is all!"
Dreamer suddenly felt lighter. To make the world
laugh? What a splendid reason to be alive!
He himself was a worrier, keeping constant watch,
but now? What fun to have Lucky as his teacher!

Lucky was also a hard worker. One day,
the bearded man noticed that a pile of discarded wood
had moved to a different place. The laughing workers pointed
to Lucky. With grim determination, he was grabbing one
plank at a time and moving it to a site close by,
finally uncovering the rabbits underneath and catching
some for his luncheonette. For loved ones must not
lose sight of their own jobs in their fascination
with another's, as people tend to do; must not
paint themselves out of the picture of life in their passion
for another, as people tend to do; must not
forget that love is giving as lavishly to the self as to another.
In the summer of life, the heat of being Together at last
can burn up the capacity to remember the self's importance.

Relationships, to shine, are equal partnerships,
as Lucky's was with the bearded man, each generous
in giving, each dwelling in the Land of Grateful for all
that they received in return, each mindful of the other.
Beholding Lucky's good fortune, Dreamer rejoiced,
glad he had found that mysterious phenomenon called
a soulmate. It was beyond Dreamer's ability to explain,
for what is a soul? He knew about mates, sort of, but souls?
Were they the invisible part of us? "Like you?"
asked Lucky. No. Not like Dreamer. Lucky saw
parts of Dreamer, the images he sent to Lucky at night.
Dreamer sensed he would never know what led the dog
to what was right for his life, someone entirely compatible,
flowers on the same stem, voices in the same wind.

Awake or asleep, Lucky smiled his sunbreak smile,
one that was never menacing, no baring of teeth,
but upturn of mouth, laughing of eyes, wagging of tail.
Seasons turned for two years, the outdoor work
turned to indoor construction, where, for safety reasons,
Lucky could not shadow his friend as he had before.
Confined to the porch outside the door, he shamelessly
inched his way over the threshold and into the heart
of the man who had looked for him every morning
        for a ritual
of patting, tummy rubbing, wrestling and dog cookies.
Shortly after the house was finished, the Scottish couple
moved to the mainland for better access to medical care.
Theirs had been Lucky's place for years, even though
his waking hours were mostly spent at the construction site.

Old feelings of abandonment flooded Lucky's
heart as they said goodby, unable to take him with them.
Did that mean the shelter again? The upturned mouth
fell as low as it could go, the happy eyes
turned worried, the summer night resounded with his cries.
Dreamer tried to block images of caged dogs,
for Dreamers never intend to scare their waking sides,
but sometimes life is frightening and full of desperation,
and sometimes that is all that is. The task of living
is facing fears, moving past them, letting better
times move in. Dreamer sent Lucky
positive images of how desolation changes:
his rescue from the shelter, healing after the accident,
meeting the bearded man, laughter, food, soulmates.

Lucky's soulmate did what soulmates do, of course.
He helped to banish the fears and give better times
a chance to move in. A call to the sheep farmer
offering Lucky a place to stay met with approval.
The farmer knew that the Scottish couple had left the island
and, more, that Lucky and the man had become inseparable.
He trusted the man to treat the dog with kindness and respect.
Dad, as the man became known, gave Lucky a home.
This one with his own room, with the washer and dryer,
this one with his own soft bed, a gift from
Mom, Dad's companion. Lucky was complete.
All his worries, only a day but feeling like a year,
were over. He climbed up on his bed and slept, dreamless.
He had a nest. His wish had come true. Yet again.

Chapter Four

AUTUMN brews magic

as Life honors, equally,

its many colors.

In cool climes, autumn's colors dazzle
the eye. Lombardy poplars shimmer in gold,
maples blush many shades of red,
echinacea heals with lavender blooms,
black-eyed susans present with pride
their deep yellow petals, purple asters
tower over garter snakes clearing
the ground of slugs, spiders, and earthworms.
Rainbow season arrives, unable to decide
whether to rain or shine, so it does both,
emblazoning in the sky every imaginable hue,
spreading a loving message from Nature itself:
keep the heart warm, especially in the cold,
embrace even the colors you do not like.

Dreamer, now that Lucky was living with a pack,
as Lucky thought of Mom and Dad and they
of him, stayed close by, sending him
dreams as needed, and Dreamers are most needed
when life changes involve living Together.
Lucky's first step into the house
came with conflict. Dad took him up
the utility porch steps, showed him a small
"doggie door" that Dad had made for him.
Painted on Lucky's face was disappointment
as he turned, raced to the front door, and looked
at Dad with pleading eyes. Dad relented.
Together was not a sometime thing. Dad
had to learn that over and over again.

Dad knew that Lucky, an outdoor dog
even if he had his own bed, had undoubtedly
never had a bath except to swim
in a nearby pond with frogs, a favorite part
of the Spring Symphony Chorus. He knew also
that feet that splashed in mud puddles dotting
the dirt driveway should stay in the utility room.
But it did not matter what Dad knew.
Lucky had inched his way across the threshold
during construction, he could inch his way
into the living room. So Dad submitted to
pawprints appearing as stenciled art on the carpet.
Couches were out of bounds, and Dreamer suggested
quite strongly that the boundaries be observed.

Once, coming up from the basement shop,
Dad found Lucky ensconced on the couch,
sleeping with all four feet in the air,
tongue lolling out of open smiling mouth,
ignoring Dreamer's warnings to *wake up!*
It happened only once; a stern word
and Lucky adapted to napping on his own bed.
Dreamer saw that the very effort to interpret
another's wishes made communication
easier. Looming conflicts faded away,
give and take galloped Together until
they actually liked to accommodate each other.
Couches remained off limits, and cars,
upholstery being rather expensive to clean.

Money and clean meant nothing, however,
when Dad heard Lucky yelping outside.
Mouth stuck open, feet sliding
on rare autumn snow, Lucky was shaking
his head, trying to oust the source of pain,
one beyond the reach of Dad's flashlight,
one that led to Lucky's first ride
in the truck, Mom's arms his seatbelt, Dad
giving Pumpkin more gas than the old truck
thought possible. It was now a rocket, no,
a swerving missile as it flew from side to side
on the slippery snow-iced surface, aimed
for the animal hospital's snow-white door.
Dad ran with the crying dog inside.

The gentle doctor extracted the culprit: a thorny
blackberry twig wedged sideways in the roof
of Lucky's very painful mouth. The surprise:
it hadn't happened sooner. Storming the bushes,
seizing branches in his mouth and casting them aside
as if they were soft down pillows, he would charge
through the brambles to the shuddering rabbits which fled
from the black and white monster of the nightmares
     that their Dreamers
were unable to block. For sometimes there is no
protection, and sometimes that is all that is.
Lucky's usual protection as he sought rabbits
in the thick of the briery bush was suddenly gone,
the snow hiding both thorn and branch,
hiding the safe passage from Lucky's view.

Lucky quieted enough after the extraction
for the vet to examine him, and the four people
it took to hold him down relaxed somewhat,
but not quite. The squirrely dog's intention
to leave that place behind was obvious.
After a rabies shot and blood test,
for no medical records existed for the dog
who had ranged freely for ten years or more,
Lucky was back in the truck, his nose out
the window where mind-expanding smells awakened
his old, innate desire for exploration,
as did a trip to town for a leash, and a visit
to Mom's hilltop house, treetops barely
reaching the second floor. An aerie, were she an eagle.

The leash stayed on. Lucky had enjoyed,
since early school years, the connection to the one
on the other end of the leash, except that now
he wanted to chase the wild turkeys on the hill,
or the grazing deer, or the neighbor's golden cat
waiting to catch a finch or two at the feeder.
Still, it was nice sitting quietly Together,
a treat after the trauma of the blackberry stick
and the veterinarian, who expressed his disbelief
that Lucky was ten, his teeth suggesting a dog
of four or five as did his seventy incredibly
strong, muscular pounds. Fresh air,
fresh food, jobs that satisfied his soul,
a fine prescription for health, thought Mom and Dad.

Dad's health resolutions excluded
field mice and other rodents, no matter
how good they were for the teeth. They were
Lucky's taste, one he would never share,
along with certain odors that spelled heaven
to Lucky, who one day rolled in the remains
of slaughtered sheep, or was it cows or pigs?
Dad did not care what it was.
He barred Lucky from the front door, sprayed him
with water and left him in an outdoor shed for the night
where Dreamer did his best to comfort him
but directed him to remove the offending aroma
if he ever intended to enter the house again.
Lucky cleaned every inch of his body.

At first light, for Dad had not slept,
as pained as Lucky at their separation from each other,
he quickly opened the shed, astounded to find
that the stench had vanished as if it had never been.
Dad rewarded Lucky with handfuls of treats.
"There is no accounting for tastes," Dreamer remarked,
"best to offer our own only if asked."
Lucky sighed. Life was not simple.
He had thought he had left rules behind.
School was their place, not in the fields or the woods,
or the ponds where he swam, or the network of holes
    that he made
when unearthing wild food for his Luncheonette,
or in Dad's house, he had thought, but no.
No sleeping on couches or rolling in guts.

Lucky had been housebroken as a young puppy;
he remembered that everything was done and left outside.
He did not remember how to ask to go out.
So he barked. Lucky's voice, once he had found it,
was very loud, holding ears loud.
Once, Dad told him to stop barking.
He did, inside house and car. Instead,
he opened and closed his mouth with a muted thump,
and Dad had to guess what he wanted. Water, a ride
in the car or the truck (a common occurrence now),
a dried salmon treat, a walk outside,
or almost anything. Life was his playground.
Obeying rules might be to placate Dad?
Might be more than that, Dreamer suggested.

No time to muse when adventures beckon.
Dad, like the Scottish man before him, was retired;
like the Scottish man, he was busier than ever.
Like the Scots of the nineteenth century,
he hauled rocks, not with sleds, but with trucks
fitted with cranes built in his shop. Granite
boulders that settlers had brought from the fields became
found treasure for his stone carving, a deep
connection with all time arising again,
each moment having its own purpose,
each part of a larger Moment, early
Scots never dreaming that their rocks would become
objects for a sculptor's chisel, or that a Border Collie
would diligently dig for rabbits under the boulders.

Beneath the Scottish man's woodshed was a haven
for rabbits until Lucky began to dig them out,
forming enormous holes. The shed's collapse
seemed imminent. Filling the gaping hollows
with boulders helped to support the structure at first,
but Lucky, undaunted, would lie on his side, using
all four feet to pull the rocks
away and force a slew of rabbits to flee.
If Lucky was almost stronger than four people,
wrestling with rocks as he mimicked the early settlers
and Dad was undoubtedly part of the reason. As was
his unflagging desire to help farmers
by ridding their fields of marauding rabbits;
it kept him working hard in the autumn of his life.

Change, however, as always, was in the air.
Excited barking at the Scottish couple's place
woke Lucky, whose naps had become more frequent.
Two dogs, Charlie (a standard poodle) and
CurlySue (part poodle, part
golden retriever), had moved next door.
No dogs had invaded his domain till now,
a fortunate happenstance, for Lucky increasingly
identified more with human beings
than with dogs, ignoring those that barked or wanted
to play or fight. Did not riding in the cab
of Pumpkin beside Dad instead of teetering
in the open truckbed like most canines
mean he was better than them? more human?

Charlie and CurlySue rode inside
their Mom's car. No ordinary canines,
in Lucky's eyes, so he tolerated them.
Dreamer, ever the staunch egalitarian,
suggested that riding inside instead of outside
meant nothing, neither was better or worse.
And being a dog was as good as being a human.
"It is just another way of being, Lucky,"
said Dreamer. "Remember, no matter what
others think, you are equal to all that is,
including dogs that ride in truckbeds,
no more important and no less."
The more Lucky pondered Dreamer's words,
the freer he was to be his own self.

Change also invaded Lucky's diet
when the neighbor showed Dad her grain-free
dog food, used for rescued wildlife
like fox and wolf, the latter an ancestor
from whom Lucky inherited a tendency
to eat quickly, as if preventing a hungry rival
from stealing his dinner. Watching Dad wolf
down his own food, he did not know
that Dad's haste was the result of many years
as a chief engineer in the Merchant Marine,
emergencies often robbing him of a meal.
Mom ate slowly, quite fearless.
For ages, mothers had been the invincible guardians
of survival; no one would dare to steal from her.

One day, Lucky's wolf heritage
surfaced blatantly. The neighbor asked Dad
to come over quickly. There was Lucky,
by her woodshed, front paws on a lineup
of seven dead rabbits, growling (unusual
for him) at Charlie and CurlySue, the wolf
snarling, "You may not steal my food."
That it was also food for eagles was forgotten
as he reverted to the wild, closing the luncheonette
for the first time, mortified later at his actions.
Dreamer reminded him of when he had robbed
the hawk of its lunch when he was not even hungry,
a sharp reminder of the pain of possessiveness,
its discomfort dispelled by the founding of the luncheonette.

Where would his hoarding of rabbits now lead?
Answers had to wait, for the woodshed, close
to ruination, became kindling for woodstoves
after Dad's truck pulled it over
before it could topple and hurt neighbor or dogs.
Lucky's Scottish-couple territory was
gone, except the house, which had never been
a nest. Best to relish the gifts he had
now; let the neighbor dogs be.
So it is in the autumn of life, old
ways disappearing as the ever-changing
present, a place of wisdom that accepts all
that is, demands attention and adaptation.
Lucky let go, made room for the new.

New was his worry about the luncheonette.
Catching rabbits was not as easy as it had been.
Those whom he had formerly served now
served him. The great horned owl began
hunting by day, joining the eagles and vultures.
Sensing his usefulness wane, Lucky sighed.
Dreamer was instantly there, a constant
friend and supporter, as was Dad.
Still, Lucky languished. When Dad was in the shop,
he slept in the warmth of the sun; when Dad appeared,
Lucky jumped up and started digging,
like a guilty employee taking too long a break.
"It is all right to be retired, Lucky,"
said Dad. "We do not have to work all the time."

Lucky's behavior made Dad laugh,
a job that mattered, as Dreamer reminded Lucky.
Dreamer and Dad loved him no matter what,
but it did not solve the dilemma of how to be useful.
"When you do not know what to do," said Dreamer,
"do not do anything. Wait for clarity."
Dreams came of racing after food
for the luncheonette, success a sometime thing.
Then quiet dreams, Dad lying under
the stars on a summer's night, Lucky beside him.
An image of Mom, sitting quietly with Lucky
on the front steps at the close of day, the silence
broken only by laughter that burst out
when Lucky licked her face. Then quiet again.

Finally, a dream of the eagles, sitting in the firs,
doing little except searching with their eyes,
moving only when an unsuspecting prey
crawled out of an apparently abandoned hole.
That was it! Waiting patiently was a skill
unknown to Lucky; he wanted to learn it.
After touring the giant holes he had dug,
he smelled a rabbit. Making not a sound,
he sat, waited, quickly snatching the luckless
rodent as it climbed out to find food,
only to become sustenance itself for whatever
hungry customer was visiting the luncheonette.
Yet another *Wow!* escaped. Life
was a game again, one he could play well.

Lucky's kind, from wolves to domestic canines,
had evolved and survived through flexibility,
like most of nature. Like juncos, winter birds
that nested on the ground, hidden by vegetation,
thwarting roaming cats by choosing instead
to nest in the hanging baskets in Mom's carport,
plants going thirsty until the babies fledged.
While Mom was protecting birds, Dad was protecting
Lucky with rules like being inside at night,
failing eyesight a threat; an unseen hole
could break the dog's leg. Lucky preferred
to cruise for midnight snacks, but Dad fretted
if Lucky did not come when called and Lucky fretted
if he caused his soulmate more worry.

That was the reason for obeying rules! Another
way to allay the fears of loved ones.
Human rules, Dreamer noted, calmed them,
like do not speed with the car (any dog
that had ever bounced back and forth in the bed
of a truck screeching around corners knew that),
and let your parents know where you are.
That was hard for Lucky, who wandered at will.
Understanding rules made it easier;
it was kinder to bark, letting Dad know
where he was, but in the darkness, Lucky
could still hide behind blackberry bushes.
Dad laughed as he chased him, but frustration
lurked beneath the laughs of the sleepy man.

Dad eventually won the game when he bought
a night vision scope that enabled him to creep
behind Lucky and grab his collar. The capture
elicited a look of mock dismay, but a night
inside with Dad made up for it, especially
when "The Rockford Files" was on, the only
television program Lucky watched. Living
intimately with Nature astonishes the heart, carries it
to unknowable realms. Having once
raised three orphaned raccoon babies,
Dad knew of their love for games, and found
the same with Lucky, but television had a strange
fascination for these non-human creatures
that mystified and entertained him.

A former neighbor told of raccoons that arrived
at her screen door at the exact same time
in the early evenings to watch a certain program
in its entirety, leaving at the end,
sated by, by...no one could guess.
Mom's sister had a dog that would watch only
tennis, her golden head following the ball
back and forth, also leaving at the end.
Lucky liked radio, too, not
the daily news but the Saturday morning program
about cars, people calling in with problems
to be solved. It was Lucky's favorite, for he shared Dad's
passion for his cars and trucks that were always ready
for action, with a little tweaking here and there:

a '46 Studebaker truck, red,
with a grill that smiled, born the same year
as Dad; a green Chevy flatbed truck
to haul boulders, destined for carving, closer
to the shop; Lucky's first love, Pumpkin,
the Ford truck that had slid to the animal hospital.
Riding in front next to Dad was always
an adventure, especially without Mom as seatbelt.
Mom was territorial about the front
in the Subaru wagon, making up for it
by spreading a quilt to warm the back seat,
a boon in autumn's colder days, though Lucky
had no seasonal stiffness like many dogs,
thanks to a daily dose of glucosamine.

What delighted Lucky was the sound of Dad's laughter
and that of the car show hosts. It became
a weekly Saturday Symphony not to be missed,
its influence much greater than Dad suspected.
Charlie and CurlySue's Mom called
one morning when Lucky was barking incessantly
at her Acura, which was making strange noises
even with the engine turned off.
When Dad lifted the hood, Lucky jumped
on top of the engine, barking, "I can do this!
I listen to the car show! I can fix it!"
To the amazement of all, Lucky sniffed and prodded,
then yelped triumphantly, pulling out the nest
of a field mouse. Another *Wow!* burst out.

Surely, Lucky had found a new job!
The car show needed his expertise!
His application to the hosts for a top position
as mechanic received no answer. Dreamer
suggested that humans knew very little
of the latent abilities of dogs, or rather chose
not to know, for if they knew it would upset
their unquenchable illusions of superiority.
Lucky laughed. "They do not even know
what I am thinking! Charlie and CurlySue
know, and Dad and Mom. Well, sometimes
they guess, but I know what they are thinking,
I know when Dad is planning to take the ferry
and whether or not he plans to take me with him."

"Humans have the ability to read the minds
of others," said Dreamer, "but choose to use words
instead. They have secrets, things to hide,
like the garlic bagels you buried so as not to hurt
Dad by rejecting his gift. Dreamers know
that opening the self to others can be fearful
for human beings, but understanding why
is quite beyond us. Dreamers see that the light
of every soul is undiminished by even
the darkest secret, unsullied by shame.
If waking sides knew their beauty, they would live
their lives accordingly, be free to read minds,
connect with Nature utterly and begin to revel
in the magic of a world that embraces without condition."

Lucky listened to Dreamer's philosophy
with half his attention, the rest on practical matters,
like running the luncheonette. The car show
forgotten, he and his colleagues worked to rout
crop-busting rabbits. The prosperity
of small farms grew. Even the smallest
of them (like Mom's, whose flowers in containers on the deck
gave way to vegetables) increased in numbers when rabbits
were not chomping on parsley and carrots and succulent peas.
Dreamer was excited by Lucky's success, and proud,
as was Dad, who bought grass-fed meat
from local farmers for Lucky to keep him strong.
The harvest was big, the customers plenty, the rabbits
in flight. Then frosts subdued the autumn colors.

Dad's advice to take time off
became increasingly attractive. One day,
the red fox, who loved nothing more
than to invade Lucky's territory and goad him to chase,
knowing he would win, accomplished his sly goal.
Lucky was a peaceable dog, averse to fighting,
never barked at another dog's challenge as if
fighting a canine was beneath him, but the fox?
From a window, Mom and Dad watched the chase.
The fox stopped by the pond to rest, aging
perhaps, like Lucky. The dog emerged
from the tall grass and suddenly both animals
were face to face, startled to stillness, neither
making a move, staring at the longtime foe.

It was as if all natural instincts
in each of them were at war with the fact that neither
wanted to fight, that chasing was fun, that maybe
seven acres was big enough for both of them.
To choose to fight could be much more than hurtful;
one of them could be killed in the fray.
The fox and the dog appeared to question their very
evolution. Old ways said fight,
win, but if one of them died, nobody won.
The new ways? The fox trotted off,
the game, for it was a game, with his newfound
friend to be resumed another day.
Lucky followed a few steps until
the fox stopped turning his head to check on him.

Mom and Dad almost forgot to breathe
as the drama unfolded and played itself out.
If two different canines could end the killing,
might humans do the same within their species?
Was it as simple as a choice not to fight?
To be open to friendships in unlikely places?
People were waging war around the globe,
old enmities dictating new violence,
hanging on, hanging on to the anger,
the fear, the grief of loss, when precious energy
could forge happier ways of being Together.
In the autumn of life, when old jobs seemed
to dwindle, Lucky had found a sublime way
of being: making peace with self and other.

With age came distressing news from a neighbor:
Lucky was on the road, his early accident forgotten.
Dad called him, but Lucky did not come.
Was it his usual selective deafness when intent
on his own way? Or had he lost his hearing,
the clatter of trucks and Dad's frantic commands
things that did not exist in a soundless world?
No accident this time, just a visit
to the vet, whom he loved personally but whose office
he dreaded. It still required four people
to hold him, still as strong as ever even if,
as tests showed, he had lost most of his hearing.
Thus Lucky became an indoor dog,
a leash restricting his former independence.

Mom and Dad worried. Would the new restraints
crush Lucky's spirit, rob him of his joyful,
exuberant will to live? Did they have a choice?
The risk of harming Lucky, the torment for a person
causing harm to him by hitting him with a car:
no choice. They must remain harmless
in a world often careless, do what they could
to ease suffering. In that mysterious space
where all beings are one, Lucky seemed
to agree, smile wide, tail wagging
with its usual abandon, appetite for scraps
and salmon treats still as keen as ever.
Nothing wrong with his endless capacity for food,
nothing wrong with his endlessly grateful mood.

Love and wonder deepened every day.
Was it living Together? Might have been.
Learning each other's ways, understanding
heightened with each conversation, deafness
requiring no words but a look was enough,
or a pat, or a wrestle on the carpet that had given up
any hopes of being clean, ever.
Lucky's enthusiasm for outings on a leash
grew even more when discovering a mutual
passion for blackberries. Lucky emulated his wolf
ancestors, front teeth removing the season's
last ripe berries, Dad and Mom
picking the sweetest from high branches, and sharing.
Wow! The entire pack was part wolf.

Chapter Five

ANOTHER WINTER

brings trust as Life reaches for

new ways of being.

The will to live can be elusive.
Easy to forget the delicate balance
it requires: the fact of equal worth
unrelated to money or talents
or what someone else says.
Or practicing love and respect even
when not feeling either, for reducing
them to feelings hides the truth:
they are not temporary matters, but rather,
all that is, all the time.
Easy to forget to extend love
and respect to the dear self, especially
in the winter of life, looking back,
remembering mistakes more than successes.

Ancient sages advise remembering
without harsh judgment, for such
criticism makes wisdom hide
like a chastised child, making it impossible
to pass it on to those who follow.
The will to live hides as well
when treating the self unkindly.
Suicides make the entire universe
mourn, it seemed to Mom and Dad,
who had known all too many who had forgotten
how beautiful they were, had forgotten that everything
changes, that they needed patience in particular;
the reason for their lives might not be revealed
until the upper reaches of age.

It did not help that human beings
were systematically destroying the environment
that was necessary for their survival, a signal
to the young that their lives meant nothing,
that only paper money had significance.
Dreamers suffered to see their pain,
but sometimes bouts of futility
depress life's wellspring
and sometimes that is all that is.
Waking sides were forgetting how
to dream their destinies alive,
how to allow new times
to heal their hearts, and needed desperately
to remember before their final chapter.

No one knew what,
if anything, Lucky had to remember.
If truth be known, his Dreamer was taking
another rest. His charge was happy;
the winter raindrops returned to play
with Lucky, and Dad took walks
no matter the weather, drying the dog
with a special towel to keep him warm.
Lucky lived in the present. Did he
remember a time before leashes?
his neighborhood friends and their gifts of food?
Lucky's Luncheonette? Did he think
about his colleagues? or the rabbits? or who
was helping the farmers? Might be.

Lucky might have remembered that while
each life has a purpose, each
moment has one as well; he made
each one count. And speaking of
counting, his allotment of salmon treats
escalated to such proportions
when he became an indoor dog
that he grew quite chunky. At least
he no longer begged for treats
from neighbors, thanks to Dad's reluctance
to engage in such a practice. The exception:
visits to Charlie and CurlySue,
whose Mom dispensed cookies, but only
after the dogs sat in a line.

When the vet suggested that Lucky go
on a diet, Dad tried to reduce
the number of handouts, but a drooping tail
always won, until Dad
realized that a corner of dried salmon
was as good as the whole. Lucky counted
the gifts; the amount was not important.
Smaller portions and extensive exercise,
though not as much as when he ran
unfettered, led to a healthy weight.
Organic vegetables from farmers who used
no pesticides (they had remembered,
life was worthwhile) helped
to keep him energetic and trim.

Preventing Lucky from eating questionable
foods in the field was not as easy.
Charlie showed Lucky how tasty
rabbit droppings could be, while Dad
leapt to stop Lucky from indulging.
Lucky introduced Charlie
to fox and cat leavings, while Dad
leapt to stop them all. Except
CurlySue, who shunned the game
but eyed Lucky with tongue hanging
down the side of her lower jaw,
undeterred by the knowledge that her love
was unrequited, circling Lucky
even though he ignored her antics.

Until Charlie died, going,
as Dreamer said, "to the other side."
That day, Lucky was kind
to CurlySue as he licked her face.
Compassion, finally, the connecting link
to other dogs, the road to respect
for them and for himself as one of them.
He even befriended a wolf spider,
bearing the name of his ancestor;
hidden in Lucky's thick fur,
it made its way inside the house
and hopped along a window sill,
looking fierce but Lucky was laughing.
Was it simply another game?

Such a privilege to be immersed
in the heart of Nature, to receive its gifts.
Maybe not the mice that cats
bring in to show their prowess
or possibly their affection.
Hard to divine the motivation
of a cat, especially when finding a kitten,
three weeks old, in the only
vent hole at the base of the house's
wall, abandoned there until Dad
gathered it up in a tee-shirt
and took it to the animal shelter
to save it from Lucky, for whom the kitten
would be a one-gulp meal.

It happened on Mother's Day, the mystery
of the kitten's mother and her sad fate
all the more poignant. The shelter
had two cats with litters; it was likely
that one would adopt the motherless, feed it
as her own. The outlook was good for the kitten.
Where was the mother? How did she feel?
Human wonderings, musing on Nature's
sorrowful moments, suddenly one
with Mothers everywhere, bestowing
care, fearful for the safety of their children,
providing for them adequately sometimes
impossible, trusting in the generosity
of adoptive mothers and fathers to know
that every creature was part of their family.

Where was Lucky's mother?
Where were his brothers, and sister?
Rumor had it that the Border Collie
who traveled every day from the north
end of the island to town, hitching
rides as he went, spending time
visiting favorite people and places,
hitching a ride back to his territory,
although all places were his territory–
rumor had it, the dog was Lucky's
brother. Both adventurous, breaking
the rules of dogs with their independence,
both trusting in the generosity
of residents to know that they were family.

Neither of them were disappointed.
Trust in life's kindness attracts
kindness. Even an abandoned kitten
learns that when brought in from the cold
and nursed by a strange cat not
its mother but yet, magically, its mother.
Even unpleasant happenings
breed kindness, Dad warning
other dog lovers to beware
the scat of a cat, a dangerous meal
for dogs, its toxins spreading disease
even among humans, a disorder
of the nervous system. Lucky's tics were
healed with timely medication.

Life's wheel turned, a tiny
growth on Lucky's back grew
to an ominous size, the biopsy
saying the dreaded word: cancer.
The veterinarian warned that subjecting
a sixteen-year-old dog
to anesthetic was a risk.
Lucky's eyes said, "Take it."
During the operation, their tears
merging with the raindrops, Mom and Dad
drove home to a silent house,
unready to ask the question: would
they ever see Lucky again?
If not, how could they stand it?

Be grateful that he had been
in their lives? Do as Lucky did,
accept what was and just go on?
Might be. Many ways
to mourn, but no comfort for a while,
nothing would stop the tears for a while.
Mom and Dad waited. And waited.
The telephone rang. He was alive.
Dad brought a cot to lay
inside of Lucky's kennel. Waiting,
as did the vet spending the night
in his office, always ready to rise
from his sleeping bag in case of need.
A paragon for his profession.

Healthy cells thrived, Lucky
went on as if he was meant to do so,
as if nothing could block his will to live.
As an elder of his tribe, he might have known
that yet another job awaited:
training loved ones to heal
the body, mind, heart, spirit.
A boy of six, wise as children
are, decided when his dog died
that dogs had shorter lives than people
because they had less to learn;
from birth, they knew how to live well.
Mom and Dad, aging with Lucky,
observed and learned, depending on him,

they realized later, in difficult times.
And times were shameful, the deeds of human
corruption, greed, cruelty, destruction,
breeding in them anger. Nay, fury,
when people left the best in them
behind to traipse after... after
the worst they had to give the world?
Those infamous pieces of green paper?
So it had been. What would evolve?
Were not some tasks impossible,
like saving the world, controlling others,
directing the evolution of a species?
They could direct their own; they set
their minds to watching Lucky more closely.

No matter what happened along
the way during his lifetime, Lucky
always created. Luncheonettes,
giant holes, new tricks.
Dad began creating. Titanium
dragons and frogs, brass artwork
for gates, steel handrails with cables
for decks to keep people safe,
stone and steel fountains to attract
bees and birds and whatever was thirsty.
And a granite sculpture, "Eye of the Beholder,"
a leaning reminder that each has
its own slant on life and each
has its own unique truth.

In the winter of the collective soul,
trust rests with the seeds of life
that awaken even in the darkest times.
Camellias bloom before winter is finished,
as do snowdrops pushing their way through frozen
ground, impatient to shout: "Trust!
Saving the world is not impossible!"
The whirlwind of energy in Lucky's pack
devoted to creation, whether sculptures,
poems, meals, gardens, paintings,
smiles–did it balance out
destruction? As if by sheer force
of will, the will to live, the ripples
of love could cover and heal the world?

Worth a try. Just in case.
In the meantime, Lucky had found a job
he could do even with sight and hearing
diminishing or maybe because they were.
His sense of smell was as sharp as ever,
leading him to places off the trail
on his walks with Dad who, thinking the pulls
on the leash were the product of blindness, pulled
back to help the dog, he thought.
Lucky began to herd Dad
to the places he wanted to sniff; instead of
pulling, he pushed, clipping Dad
on the backs of his knees, steering him
to the seductive scent, laughing as he went.

Wow! Herding was actually fun!
Mom was easy to herd. Not
outside, he seemed to know she could topple
more easily than Dad with seventy pounds
of dog pushing her off the path.
But inside? If Mom was sitting and reading,
he would park himself down at her feet
and, reverting to wolf, would stare her down,
head between paws, breaking her focus,
making her guess what he wanted. Walk?
Water? Treat? Herding sheep
was definitely a yawn, but herding people?
Rejuvenating! He felt like a puppy.
Mom and Dad felt like sheep.

Lucky's favorite herding technique
was guilt, a favorite of people as well.
But Lucky's guilt trips lost
their power over Mom and Dad
when he was still an outdoor dog.
"What? I am not coming with you?"
seemed like a teasing antic, a game.
His droop lasted only until
the car started forward. Then,
perky as ever, he trotted off
to explore a scent that wafted in the wind,
not knowing that Mom and Dad
could see him in the rear-view mirror.
It made them laugh. Dreamer, too.

Such it is in the last winter
of life, age a mirror of the young,
laughing with delight at Nature's surprises
as if for the first time. Wanting
to remember, never forget, remember
the wonder, wanting to remember the tender
connection with all living things.
Wanting to grasp a magnificent moment
changing too fast to be held
in stasis. Life was such a moment,
Mom and Dad realized with a start,
small in the arc of time. They were guests
on the planet, with room and board provided.
How lucky they were to be alive!

Then it was clear: they owned nothing.
Certainly not Lucky, who adopted Dad
as others had adopted him, finding
an old truth, that the best way
to thank someone is to do the same
for someone else. Dreamer related
such timeless sayings to Lucky as he ate
new kinds of food, Dad
cooking, Mom noting the menu
that nourished longevity: light, local
farm produce of fresh eggs,
beets, pumpkins, and fish oil
when grass-fed beef became
too rich for an aging system.

After a good meal, Lucky,
perhaps copying the use of napkins,
rolled on the carpet, wiping his mouth,
the carpet resigned by now, perhaps
even glad that the dog was content,
or rather, ecstatic with gratitude
for all that he had. He showed, by example,
how to age well: keep on
smiling courageous sunbreak smiles,
endure the hurts, illness, focus
on the companionship of loved ones,
cherish the splendor of the seasons. Embrace
even endings, which over time
open the door to new beginnings.

Lucky knew that Dreamer was
his other side, and he wanted to see him.
Dreamer was not sure it was possible.
Lucky pleaded. Inexplicably,
Dreamer appeared, white where Lucky
was black, black where white. The sparkling
eyes with a hint of mischief, both
had those, along with the radiance of compassion.
"What is it like on your side?"
asked Lucky. Dreamer smiled, told him
he would find out when the time was right.
Lucky smiled back, knowing.
It had to be wondrous, for Dreamer was wondrous.
Wow! He awoke and played with Dad.

At eighteen and a half years,
he left for his next adventure, still
playing. Echoing the early pawprints
in the electric meter's wet cement
and those on the brand new carpet,
Lucky sculpted even more
from the rain clouds in the sky. He was
there, the raindrops welcoming him
as he had welcomed them. He was
there, as he was in the heart of his soulmate,
as he was in the firs with the elegant eagles.
Lucky was one with all that he loved,
in timeless remembering, making his mark,
finding peace in the Land of Grateful.

Together is the answer, Lucky seemed
to be saying, telling his story from the circle
of life and death that gently transforms
opposites to oneness. Love, the narrator
of all stories, energizes everything,
nothing more or less, careening
through space and time like an old truck
racing to heal with the urgent message
that no one is ever alone,
that every single thing is beauty
connecting every single heart.
Such is the path to the will to live.
For always, joy abides in wholeness,
and always, that is all that is.

THE END

Acknowledgements

Lucky to be Alive: A Love Story is a work of fiction. Lucky, a real Border Collie, was the inspiration for the story as it followed him through the seasons of life. Also real were the many people who helped to bring the book into being. A heartfelt thank-you to:

Emily Reed, the editor for the book, for her clear and constructive suggestions, and for her warm and supportive friendship;

Ian Byington of By Design, for the benefits of his talent, gentle guidance, and humor as he designed and put together the book;

playwright Ernest Pugh, who read early drafts with an artist's eye and who shared freely his tomes on writing poetry;

writer and naturalist Susan Vernon, who read the book for its accuracy in her field and helped to proof it as well;

many colleagues and friends, some of whom read early drafts and provided invaluable feedback, and all of whom not only provided moral support and encouragement but also were always good for a laugh, including, among others, Jacki Altier, Alan Boyne, Deb Bruels, Lorna Dittmer, Louise Dustrude, Jean Hendrickson, Barbara Martin, Jim McCormick, John Orders, Tom Phillips, Lee Sturdivant, and Janet Thomas.

A heartfelt thank-you also goes to Lucky's special friends:

Rex and Lisa Guard, without whom we would not have met Lucky;

Nancy Clifton, friend, neighbor, and a font of information about the canine world;

G. James Lehocky, DVM, for his kind and enthusiastic care of Lucky for so many years;

Dodie Gann, whose generous donation of agricultural land to the San Juan Preservation Trust honored both the history and the future of working farms such as those Lucky knew, protecting their existence for generations to come.

Family, past and present, far and near, are too numerous to name, but I treasure them. To my late parents, from whom I inherited a respect for the wisdom of the natural world and a dedication to the equality of self and other, a profound thank-you for enriching my life.

Always and ever, my love and gratitude go to Jeff Brash, the caring, creative, and adventurous man who has been my companion for almost two decades and who treated me to stories of Lucky's antics on a daily basis; and to Lucky. During the ten years that we spent with him, his most important job, it seemed, was to make us laugh. We are both grateful to him for teaching us, by his example, what it takes to be in love with life.

About the Author

Wendy E. Shepard grew up amid the woods, fields, and small family farms of New England. She received an AB degree in English from Radcliffe College, with special attention to dramatic literature, and an MS degree from the Bank Street College of Education, immersing herself in the study of creative human development.

After thirty years of working in the arts and education in New York City and Los Angeles, she migrated to the Pacific Northwest to write. Her plays have appeared in juried festivals and her articles in a variety of publications.

She lives on an island amid woods, fields, and small family farms.

CPSIA information can be obtained at www.ICGtesting.com
Printed in the USA
BVOW042008290513

321940BV00001B/14/P